planet EARTH
Earth's Water Cycle

By Amy Bauman

Science curriculum consultant: Suzy Gazlay, M.A.,
science curriculum resource teacher

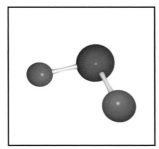

 Gareth Stevens
Publishing

Please visit our web site at www.garethstevens.com.
For a free catalog describing our list of high-quality books, call 1-800-542-2595 (USA)
or 1-800-387-3178 (Canada). Our fax: 1-877-542-2596

Library of Congress Cataloging-in-Publication Data available upon request from the publisher.

ISBN-13: 978-0-8368-8919-2 (lib. bdg.)
ISBN-10: 0-8368-8919-3 (lib. bdg.)
ISBN-13: 978-0-8368-8926-0 (softcover)
ISBN-10: 0-8368-8926-6 (softcover)

This North American edition first published in 2008 by
Gareth Stevens Publishing
A Weekly Reader® Company
1 Reader's Digest Road
Pleasantville, NY 10570-7000 USA

This U.S. edition copyright © 2008 by Gareth Stevens, Inc. Original edition copyright © 2007 by ticktock Media Ltd.
First published in Great Britain in 2007 by ticktock Media Ltd., Unit 2, Orchard Business Centre, North Farm Road,
Tunbridge Wells, Kent, TN2 3XF United Kingdom

ticktock Project Editor: Ruth Owen
ticktock Picture Researcher: Lizzie Knowles
ticktock Project Designer: Emma Randall
With thanks to: Suzy Gazlay, Mark Sachner, and Elizabeth Wiggans

Gareth Stevens Editor: Jayne Keedle
Gareth Stevens Creative Director: Lisa Donovan
Gareth Stevens Graphic Designer: Alex Davis
Gareth Stevens Cover Designer: Yin Ling Wong

Photo credits (t = top; b = bottom; c = center; l = left; r = right):
Alamy: 29 main. FLPA: 13bl. Corbis: 11cr, 16–17main. Mike Dawson: cover. Getty Images: 20t, 27l. iStockphoto: 29 cr.
Johnny Johnson: 10–11 main. Jiang Kehong/Xinhua Press/Corbis: 16–17 main. Daniel Kerek/Alamy: 12 main NASA: 5tc,
9bl, 17br. NHPA: 16bl. PlanetObserver – www.planetobserver.com: 6cl. Rex Features: 28 all. Shutterstock: title page all,
contents page, 4l, 4tc, 4cc, 4bc, 4–5 main, 5tr, 5cr, 5br, 6tl, 6bl, 6–7 main, 7b, 8–9 main, 9tr, 9br, 10tl, 10cl. 10bl, 11c,
14tl, 14cl, 14–15 main, 15b, 16tl, 16cl, 18tl, 18cl, 18bl, 18–19 main, 19b, 20cl, 20bl, 21b, 22tl, 22bl, 23 main, 26clt,
26clb, 26 main, 27tr, 27cr, 29tr, 30 all, 31 all. Science Photo Library: 12tl, 12cl, 12bl, 19tr. Superstock: 9cr, 22br. ticktock
media archive: 4bl, 7tr, 13t, 15t, 21 map, 23r.

Every effort has been made to trace copyright holders, and we apologize in advance for any omissions. We would be pleased
to insert the appropriate acknowledgments in any subsequent edition of this publication.

Printed in the United States of America

1 2 3 4 5 6 7 8 9 10 09 08 07

CONTENTS

CHAPTER 1:
The Blue Planet

We swim in it. We bathe in it. Our landscape is carved and changed by it. Sometimes it pours from the sky. Sometimes it falls as snow. It's water. Without it, plants, animals, and people could not survive!

WATER WORLD

Earth is often called the Blue Planet. There's a good reason for this. More than 70 percent of Earth's surface is covered with water. Scientists have found some evidence showing that Mars may have had liquid water in the past. As far as we know, however, Earth is the only planet in the solar system that has water.

Plants absorb water through their leaves and roots.

Doctors say we should drink at least eight glasses of water each day.

Like humans, zebras and all other animals need water to survive.

For many living things, including fish, water is home!

We depend on lakes and other large bodies of water in many ways. Some lakes provide us with fresh drinking water. They may also contain fish and other animals we eat.

H₂O: THE WATER MOLECULE

OXYGEN

HYDROGEN

All substances are made of tiny particles called **molecules**. Each molecule is made up of even smaller particles called atoms. The atoms contain the chemicals that make up that substance. H_2O is the scientific symbol for water. The H tells us that water contains the gas hydrogen. The O tells us that water contains another gas, oxygen. The 2 after the H tells us that each water molecule has two atoms of hydrogen for every one atom of oxygen.

Did you know that the same water that existed on Earth at the time of the dinosaurs is still on Earth today? That's because the amount of water on Earth doesn't change. The water keeps moving around and around in an endless cycle.

Water is found in oceans, rivers, and streams. It is frozen in giant masses of ice at the North and South poles. People use pumps to bring underground water up to the surface. Plants draw up water through their roots. High above the surface, water gathers in rain clouds. It falls to Earth as rain, snow, and **hail**.

All living things on Earth need water. You could go weeks without food. You could survive for only about a week without water! In fact, you are made mostly of water. About 70 percent of an adult's body is water.

WATER AND YOU

WATER AT WORK
Inside your body, water carries substances to the parts where they are needed. Water transports oxygen and nutrients from your food. It also keeps your skin moist and carries away waste.

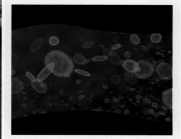

A KEY INGREDIENT
Blood (above) is 83 percent water. Your brain is 75 percent water. Even your bones are 25 percent water!

WATER WAYS
You can get some of the water you need from food. Fruits and vegetables contain lots of water. A watermelon is more than 95 percent water!

THE LARGEST OCEAN

The Pacific is Earth's largest ocean. It covers 60,060,894 square miles (155,557,000 square kilometers). That's greater than the area of all the dry land on Earth.

CASPIAN SEA

LARGEST SALTWATER LAKE

The world's largest saltwater lake is the Caspian Sea. It is partly in Europe and partly in Asia. The sea covers 149,190 square miles (386,400 sq km).

THE SALTIEST SEA

The Dead Sea, between Israel and Jordan, is the saltiest body of water in the world. Its water is nine times saltier than most seawater. The salt makes the water very dense, so it's easy for people to float in the water.

EARTH'S SALT WATER

About 97 percent of Earth's water is in the oceans and seas. Many scientists agree that there are five oceans around the world. They all link together to form a single, large mass of **salt water**. Seas are also connected to the oceans. Seas are smaller, shallower areas of salt water.

SALTY OCEANS AND SEAS

Seawater is mostly hydrogen and oxygen. Both are **elements**—they contain just one type of atom. Water contains small amounts of other elements. Two of these are sodium and chlorine. They make up the salt we sprinkle on our food. As rivers flow to the sea, they carry soil and rock. Soil and rock also contain many elements, including sodium and chlorine. When the river meets the ocean, some of the soil and rocks fall to the ocean bed. But the salts dissolve, or become mixed into the water. That is what makes oceans and seas salty.

Far beneath the ocean's surface lie deep ocean trenches. Some are so deep that the tallest mountains on the surface could easily fit in them. The seafloor is also lined with tall volcanoes and vast underwater mountain ranges. Humans have explored less than 10 percent of the oceans' depths.

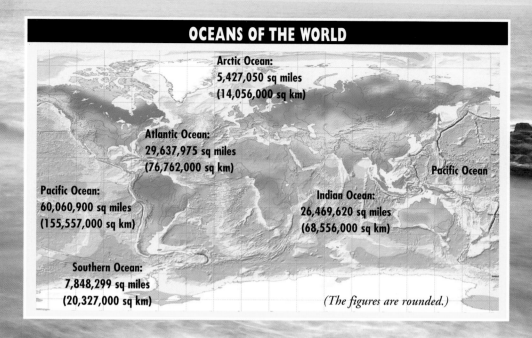

OCEANS OF THE WORLD

Arctic Ocean:
5,427,050 sq miles
(14,056,000 sq km)

Atlantic Ocean:
29,637,975 sq miles
(76,762,000 sq km)

Pacific Ocean

Pacific Ocean:
60,060,900 sq miles
(155,557,000 sq km)

Indian Ocean:
26,469,620 sq miles
(68,556,000 sq km)

Southern Ocean:
7,848,299 sq miles
(20,327,000 sq km)

(The figures are rounded.)

THE OCEANS AT WORK

The temperatures of the **atmosphere** (the air surrounding Earth) and the land are affected by heat from the Sun. The temperature of the oceans is affected in the same way. Shallow water in hot areas, such as the Persian Gulf, can be as warm as 96.8° Fahrenheit (36° Celsius). However, deep water is much cooler. Most ocean water is between 32° and 37.4° F (0° and 3° C). Air and water currents circulate the Sun's heat around the globe. That helps keep ocean temperatures from being extremely cold during the winter or extremely hot during the summer.

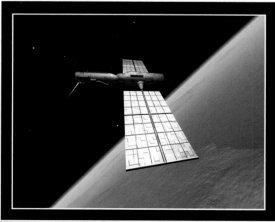

STUDYING THE OCEANS

Satellites orbit, or circle, our planet hundreds of miles above Earth's surface. Today, instruments on satellites can measure the surface temperature of the ocean to within a half a degree. They can provide information on winds, wave heights, and even where fish can be found. A ship might take weeks or months to travel across the globe. Satellites, however, can give us information about all the world's oceans in just a few days.

WATER ON EARTH

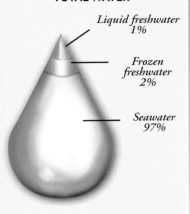

TOTAL WATER

Liquid freshwater
1%

Frozen
freshwater
2%

Seawater
97%

EARTH'S FRESHWATER

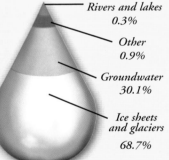

Rivers and lakes
0.3%

Other
0.9%

Groundwater
30.1%

Ice sheets
and glaciers
68.7%

EARTH'S FRESHWATER

Only 3 percent of the water on Earth is **freshwater**. That means the water is not salty. About 1 percent is liquid freshwater that plants, humans, and animals can use.

LIQUID FRESHWATER

Liquid freshwater is found in lakes, rivers, streams, and ponds. Freshwater is also found underground. In fact, there is 100 times more freshwater underground than in all of Earth's rivers and lakes put together. This **groundwater** is stored in **aquifers**. An aquifer is a natural underground lake. Water seeps into the ground and is stored between layers of gravel and rock particles. It is also stored in **permeable** rock. Water can move through permeable rock. The rock is like a bath sponge but much harder!

FROZEN FRESHWATER

About two-thirds of Earth's freshwater is frozen in **glaciers** and in the **polar ice caps**.

About 10 percent of Earth's land is covered with glaciers. These vast, slow-moving masses of frozen ice can range in size from a football field to more than 100 miles (160 km) long. Some of the water on Earth has been frozen for a very long time. Ice at the base of the ice caps in the Canadian Arctic is more than 100,000 years old.

The Hubbard Glacier in Alaska stretches 76 miles (122 km). Its front edge, or face, is more than 6 miles (10 km) wide. As the glacier slowly moves, it changes the landscape around it.

THE GREAT LAKES

The Great Lakes are five freshwater lakes on the border between the United States and Canada. The lakes and their connecting rivers make up Earth's largest freshwater system. The lakes contain 20 percent of the world's freshwater. If the water in the Great Lakes were spread across the United States, the country would be covered with more than 9 feet (2.7 meters) of water!

SUPERIOR

HURON

ONTARIO

MICHIGAN

ERIE

FRESHWATER RECORDS

LONGEST RIVER
The Nile River in Africa is the world's longest river. It measures 4,145 miles (6,670 km).

GREATEST RIVER BY VOLUME
The Amazon River in South America has more water flowing in it than any other river on Earth. One-fifth of all the world's river water flows in the Amazon. It pours 40,000 gallons (151,416 liters) of water into the Atlantic Ocean every second.

LARGEST LAKE BY VOLUME
Lake Baikal in Russia is the world's largest freshwater lake by volume. It contains about 20 percent of the freshwater on Earth.

Water is one of many natural substances found on Earth. Some natural substances are gases. Others are liquids or solids. Many natural substances are found in one of these three states of **matter** and can be changed into another. Water is the only substance that can be found in all three states of matter in the natural environment.

LIQUID
Water is in its liquid state when its temperature is between 32° F and 212° F (1° C and 100° C).

GAS
When its temperature rises above 212° F (100° C), water changes into a gas called **water vapor**—which we sometimes see as steam.

SOLID
When its temperature drops to 32° F (0° C), water freezes into ice.

CHAPTER 2:
Water, Water Everywhere

All the water that has ever been on Earth is still on Earth today. All the water we will ever be able to use is on the planet or in the atmosphere right now.

AN ENDLESS CYCLE
The water on our planet is constantly being recycled in a huge process called the water cycle. Think about the water you drank today. It could be the same water that your grandfather drank as a boy. Maybe it was the same water Michelangelo used to wash his paintbrushes 500 years ago! Water moves from the oceans and lakes up into the atmosphere, down to the land, and back again. Many factors can upset the balance of the water cycle.

Icebergs are large chunks of ice that have broken off from glaciers. They are made of frozen freshwater. The Arctic region produces up to 50,000 icebergs a year. The Antarctic region produces too many to count!

We cannot increase the amount of water on our planet. If the water cycle is upset, all living things on Earth will be affected. That's why it's important to understand water and how the water cycle works.

A SPECIAL SUBSTANCE

Water is special. It is the only substance found naturally in three different states of matter. It can be a liquid, a gas, or a solid. Water can change easily from one form to another. Water's ability to change forms makes the water cycle possible.

Did you enjoy a glass of water today? Perhaps that mouthful of water was last used by an elephant taking a bath!

ICE ON TOP

When most liquids cool, the molecules they are made from squeeze together more tightly. That makes the liquid more dense. But water behaves differently from all other liquids. Water molecules expand as they freeze. Therefore, ice is much less dense than liquid water. That is why ice floats on water. This is good news for fish and water animals. They can live in the water under the floating ice.

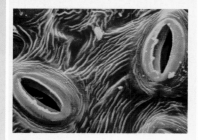

TRANSPIRATION

Plants give off water vapor through pores (tiny holes) in their leaves. This process is called **transpiration**. This image shows plant pores, called stomates, magnified 715 times under a microscope.

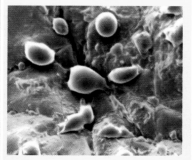

PERSPIRATION

Perspiration, or sweat, is one way that humans put water vapor into the air. The image above shows beads of sweat on skin. The image has been magnified 15 times.

BREATHING

On a cold day, you can see water vapor in your breath. We lose about 8.5 ounces (250 milliliters) of water from our bodies every day just by breathing.

THE WATER CYCLE — EVAPORATION

Water enters the water cycle from many different sources. Heat from the Sun constantly warms water on Earth's surface and turns liquid water into water vapor. The invisible gas then rises into the sky and is absorbed into the atmosphere. That part of the water cycle is called **evaporation**.

WHERE DOES THE WATER COME FROM?

About 80 percent of the water vapor in air comes from the oceans. Water also evaporates from lakes and rivers. It even evaporates from the ground. The next time you see a small puddle on the sidewalk near your home, you may notice that it soon disappears when the Sun shines. That's because the water has evaporated. Water evaporates faster on a hot day than on a cold day, but evaporation happens all the time.

Plants, animals, and people also add water vapor to the air. When people or animals breathe out, they release water vapor into the atmosphere.

Earth's atmosphere protects us from the Sun's harmful rays. However, it lets enough of the Sun's heat energy through to evaporate water. Heat from the Sun drives the water cycle.

THE WATER CYCLE

2. VAPOR COOLS AND TURNS TO WATER

*The warm water vapor rises. Mountains and hills direct air currents upward, where temperatures are cooler. There, the water vapor cools further. The vapor condenses into tiny water droplets, which we see as clouds. That change is called **condensation**.*

3. RAINDROPS FALL TO THE GROUND

*Slowly, the water droplets bunch together. The drops get bigger and heavier until they fall to the ground as rain. Rain, snow, sleet, hail, and fog are all types of **precipitation**.*

1. THE SUN HEATS SURFACE WATER

*Heat from the Sun turns water on Earth's surface into vapor. That process is called **evaporation**. Most of the water in the air comes from the ocean, but it also evaporates from lakes, ponds, and rivers. Even plants and animals release water vapor into the air.*

4. RAINWATER FLOWS INTO LAKES AND THE SEA

*The water falls into rivers and streams. Some water sinks into the ground. Most rainwater flows downhill to the sea. When precipitation gathers on Earth's surface, it is ready to start the cycle all over again. The process of water gathering is called **accumulation**.*

TRANSPIRATION

A plant absorbs water from the soil through its roots. The water is carried through the plant through very thin tubes. The water delivers moisture and nutrients to the plant. Eventually the plant gives off water vapor from its leaves. This process is called transpiration. **Humidity** is a measure of the amount of water vapor in the air. Rain forests are very humid. This is because they have so many plants, and the plants are all giving off water vapor.

CONDENSATION IN ACTION

DEW

Dew is water that condenses at ground level on warm nights. As the ground gets cold, the air cools, too. Warm water vapor condenses on grass, rocks, and other surfaces.

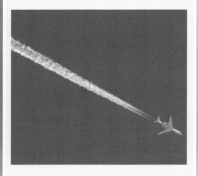

CONTRAILS

The trails that planes sometimes leave behind them are known as contrails. That name is short for "condensation trails." These cloud-like trails occur when water vapor in the hot exhaust from the plane meets cold air at high altitudes. The hot water vapor condenses into liquid cloud droplets.

ALL STEAMED UP!

Have you noticed that people's eyeglasses sometimes steam up? That can happen if a person goes from a cold place to a warm one. Warm water vapor in the air meets the cool surface of the glasses and condenses into water droplets.

THE WATER CYCLE — CONDENSATION

As warm water vapor rises, winds move it around in the atmosphere. Mountains and hills also force air currents upward. The water vapor rises higher and higher. With all that evaporation, you might think the atmosphere would contain a lot of water. But less than 1 percent of the atmosphere is made up of water vapor.

Water vapor rises high into the atmosphere, where temperatures are colder. As the water vapor cools, it becomes drops of liquid water again. The change back to a liquid is called **condensation**.

Clouds look light and fluffy, but an average cloud weighs as much as a jumbo jet! The warm air that carried the water vapor up also helps keep the cloud in the air.

MAKING CLOUDS

The droplets of water begin to collect. They gather around dust, salt, and other tiny particles in the air. We see these gatherings of water droplets as clouds. Even when there are no clouds, the vapor is there. The droplets are just too small to be seen.

Millions of these cloud droplets are needed to form just one raindrop. Eventually, the drops get bigger and heavier. The clouds become saturated. That means they have as many droplets as they can hold. When they become big and heavy, they fall to the ground.

HOW QUICKLY DOES WATER EVAPORATE?

Materials needed
- a wide, shallow container
- water
- a narrow, deeper container

1) Pour half a cup of water into each of the containers.

2) Place both containers in a warm, sunny place.

3) After a few hours, compare the amount of water in each container. What do you observe?

The evaporation rate of water depends on several factors. One of these is the amount of surface area open to the air. On a hot, sunny day, water from a wide, shallow lake evaporates more quickly than water in a narrower, deeper lake.

INVESTIGATING CONDENSATION

Materials needed
- two glasses or jars
- room-temperature water
- ice water

1) Fill one glass with room-temperature water. Fill the other glass with ice water.

2) What do you observe?

You should see drops of condensation form on the outside of the glass filled with ice water. Warm water vapor condenses when it comes into contact with something cold, such as ice.

Snowflakes always have six sides. No two snowflakes are alike.

Raindrops really ARE shaped like drops. The force of gravity on the raindrops "drags" them into a drop form. Without gravity acting on them, raindrops would be more rounded.

THE WATER CYCLE — PRECIPITATION

The cooler the air gets, the less moisture it is able to hold. The gathering water soon becomes heavy enough to fall back to Earth. That is called **precipitation**. Rain is the most common form of precipitation. But the moisture can also take the form of snow, hail, and **sleet**. All are types of precipitation.

RAIN AND SNOW

Raindrops form when colliding cloud droplets combine. Snowflakes form when the air temperature falls below freezing at 32° F (0° C). The cloud droplets turn into ice crystals. As more water freezes on the ice crystals, they grow bigger. The crystals fall through the clouds, bumping into other crystals on the way. That is how snowflakes form.

The speed at which rain falls depends on the size of the raindrops. Heavy rain can fall at speeds of up to 35 miles (56 km) per hour!

OUT OF BALANCE

Different places receive different amounts of rain. But sometimes an area will receive no rain or less rain than usual. Too little rain can cause a **drought**. People and animals cannot find water to drink. Crops cannot grow. That can lead to severe food shortages, or **famine**. Too much rain can cause floods. Rivers can overflow their banks. Sometimes **flash floods** occur when the ground cannot soak up the rain quickly enough. Floods can wipe out crops, damage homes, and cost lives.

BACK DOWN TO EARTH

Over time, the amount of water that falls as precipitation across the globe is exactly the same as the amount that evaporates. Water that falls in the ocean has completed the water cycle. Water that falls on the land, however, still has a way to go to complete its cycle.

RAINFALL RECORDS

GREATEST 24-HOUR DOWNPOUR

The record for the greatest rainfall during a single 24-hour period goes to a town on Réunion. This small island is located off the east coast of Africa. On January 7–8, 1966, the town received 72 inches (183 centimeters) of rain.

MOST RAIN IN A YEAR

The greatest rainfall in one place in a year was recorded at Cherrapunji, India. In 1861, the city got 905 inches (2,300 cm) of rain.

WORLD'S RAINIEST PLACE

One of the world's rainiest places is Mount Waialeale (WHY-ah-lay-ah-lay). It is located on Kauai, one of the Hawaiian islands. The mountain's annual rainfall is about 449 inches (1,140 cm). As warm air passes over the island, it meets the steep sides of the mountain and rises quickly. That creates a lot of condensation. As a result, a lot of rain falls in a small area.

MOUNT WAIALEALE

KAUAI

STREAMS AND RIVERS
Small trickles of water move downhill and join bigger flows. Channels and valleys in Earth's surface become gathering places for moving water. These gathering places become rivers that constantly move downhill toward the oceans.

GROUNDWATER AND UNDERGROUND STREAMS
Water in aquifers slowly trickles downhill between cracks in underground rocks. This water may become an underground stream. Eventually it will join a body of water on the surface.

LAKES AND PONDS
Gravity keeps water constantly moving downward. But the uneven surface of Earth traps water in dips, where it forms ponds or lakes.

THE WATER CYCLE — ACCUMULATION

Every raindrop or snowflake that falls to Earth is on its way to join the final stage of the water cycle. The gathering of water back on Earth is called **accumulation**. Some water that falls on land will run off into streams, rivers, and lakes. Some water will be absorbed and become groundwater in aquifers.

WATER ON THE MOVE

Gravity keeps water moving down toward the oceans. Melting snow flows down mountains and forms streams. Rivers and streams flow across the land to join the sea. Groundwater moves slowly underground to join rivers or to flow into the ocean.

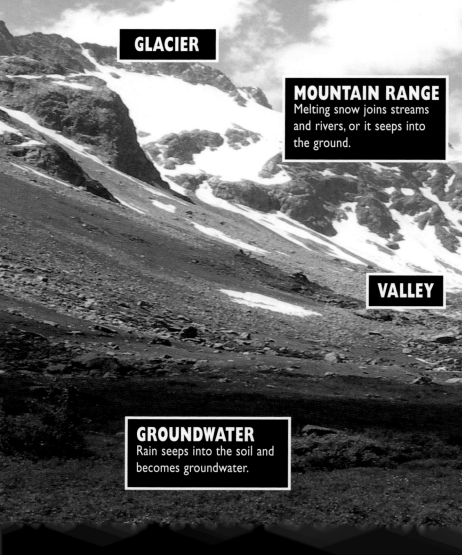

GLACIER

MOUNTAIN RANGE
Melting snow joins streams and rivers, or it seeps into the ground.

VALLEY

GROUNDWATER
Rain seeps into the soil and becomes groundwater.

No matter where it falls, all water will eventually make its way back to the oceans. That completes one part of the water cycle.

REJOINING THE WATER CYCLE

Rain that falls on a warm day could rejoin the water cycle almost immediately, by evaporating again. But not all water that falls on Earth rejoins the cycle so fast. Some water seeps deep underground. It could stay there for thousands of years. Some snowflakes freeze and stay trapped in a glacier for hundreds of years. A drop of water at the bottom of the ocean could be there for centuries before it reaches the water's surface, evaporates, and rejoins the cycle. A water molecule can spend millions of years at the accumulation stage.

MELTDOWN!

Global warming is the gradual warming of Earth. As temperatures increase, ice stored in Earth's glaciers will begin to melt. If all the ice stored in glaciers melted, Earth's oceans would rise by about 230 feet (70 m)! Many towns and cities around the world are built at sea level or just above sea level. This means the land they are built on is at the same level as the ocean's surface. A rise in the water level of just 10 feet (3 m) would mean that cities such as London and New York would be underwater.

RIVER
A river winds across the land until it joins the ocean.

OCEAN

STREAM
A mountain stream will eventually join a river.

The Amazon rain forest in South America can contain up to 1,500 different plant species in an area the size of just two football fields.

At night, the desert gets cold. Water vapor in the air condenses into water on the spikes of plants, such as the saguaro cactus. The water then trickles onto the ground to be collected by the plant's roots.

Camels live in hot deserts. A camel can drink 32 gallons (121 liters) of water at one time. It can then go a week or longer without any water at all!

DISTRIBUTION OF EARTH'S WATER

Water is not distributed equally over Earth's land. Some parts of the world receive rain almost every day. Others may go weeks, months, or even years without rain. Water is an essential factor to all life on Earth. Access to water affects the number and types of plants and animals that a place can support.

WATER TO SPARE

As the Sun shines down on the plants and trees of a rain forest, huge amounts of water vapor rise into the atmosphere. In turn, this creates huge amounts of rain. Rain forests are home to millions of different plants and animals because water is plentiful.

LIMITED WATER SUPPLIES

Deserts are places that get less than 10 inches (about 25 cm) of rainfall each year. Fewer animals and plants can survive there. Desert animals and plants have adapted to deal with a limited water supply. Some desert plants, such as the saguaro cactus, have spiky leaves with very little surface area. The small size of the leaves stops too much water from evaporating from the plant.

WATER AND BIOMES

We separate the world into large regions called **biomes**. Each type of biome has a particular kind of weather and climate. Plants, animals, and people adapt their lives according to the amount of water in the biome where they live.

EARTH'S BIOMES

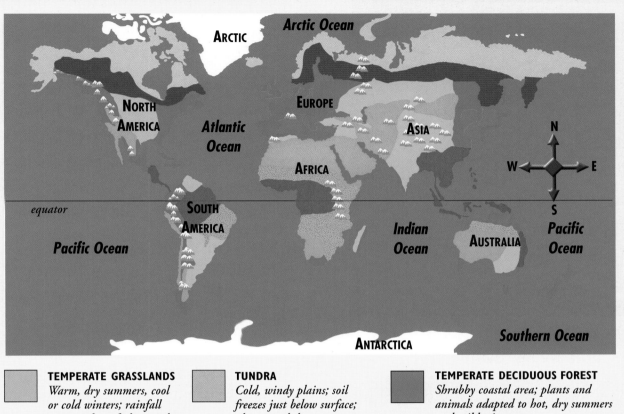

ARCTIC · **Arctic Ocean**
NORTH AMERICA · *Atlantic Ocean* · **EUROPE** · **ASIA**
AFRICA
equator
SOUTH AMERICA · *Indian Ocean* · **AUSTRALIA** · *Pacific Ocean*
Pacific Ocean
N · W · E · S
Southern Ocean
ANTARCTICA

 TEMPERATE GRASSLANDS
Warm, dry summers, cool or cold winters; rainfall supports lots of plant and animal life

 TUNDRA
Cold, windy plains; soil freezes just below surface; plants need short roots to absorb nutrients

 TEMPERATE DECIDUOUS FOREST
Shrubby coastal area; plants and animals adapted to hot, dry summers and mild winters

 SAVANNA
Large plains with scattered trees and bushes; amount of plant life determined by amount of rainfall

ARCTIC/ANTARCTICA
Extremely cold and dry all year; frozen ground and icy seas; little plant life

 CONIFEROUS FOREST
Cold evergreen forest; most animals migrate or hibernate in winter

 DESERT
Dry land, little rain; plant life includes cacti, which store water

 OCEAN
Saltwater environment supports a huge variety of marine life

TROPICAL RAIN FOREST
Hot, wet climate that supports a huge variety of life

Precipitation is low in the Arctic. Most precipitation falls as snow. Arctic animals, such as polar bears, are surrounded by salt water and ice, so they rarely drink. They have adapted to get the water they need from their food.

Water, with the help of the wind, shapes cliffs and shores along a Hawaiian coast. The Na Pali coast of the island of Kauai is known for its breathtaking cliffs.

CHAPTER 3:
Water in Action

The water cycle is all about water changing between states of matter. During the cycle, water changes from a liquid to a gas and back again. Sometimes it also becomes a solid. As Earth's water goes through this process, plants, animals, and people use the water in its three states. The water is also busy changing the face of Earth.

SHAPING OUR WORLD

The oceans pull and push at the edges of the land. The water reshapes whole coastlines and cuts craggy cliffs into them.

The ground and rocky **landforms**, such as mountains, are weathered and eroded by rainwater or river water. That means they are worn away until they become crumbly. The material that is cut away by the water is called **sediment**. The rainwater or river water carries the sediment to a new place.

Over millions of years, rivers have carved V-shaped valleys into the land. Frozen water in the form of glaciers slowly moves over Earth's surface, leaving behind U-shaped valleys.

A U-shaped glacial valley in Switzerland

The Grand Canyon in Arizona was carved from the surrounding rock by the Colorado River. In its deepest places, the gorge is 5,906 feet (1,800 m) deep.

*Water movement below Earth's surface causes **erosion**, too. Here water has carved out a large underground cave. Water running underground can create incredible features, such as stalactites (seen above). They look like icicles, but they are really rock formations. They form when water with calcium drips. The calcium hardens and builds up over time.*

HOW DOES WATER SHAPE THE LAND?

Materials needed

- a rectangular tray with sides
- water
- two wooden blocks
- sand

1) Fill the tray with the sand.

2) Set one end of the tray on the wooden blocks so the tray is sitting at a slant.

3) Slowly pour a stream of water into the tray at the high end. What do you observe?

> ⓘ Even a small, slow trickle of water has the power to make changes to Earth's surface. These changes can happen quickly, for example, during a flood. Or they can happen gradually over millions of years.

4) Experiment with shaping the "land." Place objects in the path of your stream of water. Use some lightweight objects and some heavy objects. Observe what happens.

5) Vary the amount of water you pour in the sand. Try a trickle of water. Then try pouring a lot of water in at one time. Observe what happens.

WATER AT WORK

LIVESTOCK FARMING

Water is needed to raise livestock, such as sheep, cows, and chickens. A dairy cow needs to drink nearly 5 gallons (19 liters) of water to produce only about 1 gallon (3.8 liters) of milk.

INDUSTRIAL USES

Factories use water in many ways as part of the manufacturing process. Water is used in making goods, for washing, and for cooling equipment. Water is also used to transport finished products by ship. About 300 million gallons (1.135 billion liters) of water are used every day to produce all the newspapers printed in the United States.

HUMAN USES OF WATER

People have always needed water to drink and for survival. We use water for washing, growing crops, and raising animals. In addition to those basic needs, people use water for transportation and shipping goods. Look at a world map and see how many major cities are built close to the ocean. Look at how many more are near major rivers and lakes. About 90 percent of all goods traded between countries are still transported by ships.

ADVANCES WITH WATER

Modern technology has helped us find new ways to make water work for us. Huge dams change the course of rivers and collect the water in **reservoirs**. The water passes through a system that purifies, or cleans, the water. This system removes disease-causing **organisms**, chemicals, and **pollutants**. Then the clean water is pumped directly to our homes.

Temperate biomes have enough natural rainfall to grow crops. Today, we can grow crops even in hot, dry places that have little rainfall. Water is pumped from rivers, lakes, reservoirs, and wells to irrigate crops. About 60 percent of the world's freshwater is used in **irrigation**.

We use water for fun, too! Cruise ships and sailboats dot our oceans. Swimming pools and hot tubs are great places to relax.

Hydroelectric power plants are built over flowing rivers. First, the water is stored behind a dam. Then, as the water is released, its movement turns huge turbine blades. The energy of the flowing water generates electricity.

WASTEWATER

Waste from animals passes back into the ground naturally. Human waste and dirty water usually travel to sewage treatment plants through underground pipes. At the treatment plant, bulky waste is removed. The water then passes through different tanks. Each tank contains tiny organisms. They digest and break down the sewage until it is harmless. When the water is clean, it is returned to a river or to the sea.

Here are some common uses of water in the home. Also shown is the average amount of water each activity uses.

- One bath: 21 gallons (80 liters)
- One shower: 9.2 gallons (35 liters)
- One toilet flush: 2 gallons (7.6 liters)
- One dishwasher load: 6.6 gallons (25 liters)
- One washing machine load: 17.2 gallons (65 liters)

Calculate how much water you use in a single day.

AVERAGE USES OF WATER IN THE HOME

Laundry and dishes 20%

Drinking and cooking 5%

Toilets 45%

Bathing 30%

CHAPTER 4: Saving Water

Water is an important natural resource. It is essential to the survival of all life on Earth. Water is so much a part of our everyday lives, however, that we can easily take it for granted.

WASTING WATER

Do you have any faucets in your home that drip? One drip per second means that more than 1 gallon (3.8 liters) of water a day is escaping from your faucet. Do you leave the tap running when you brush your teeth? Running a tap for just one minute can use about 2.6 gallons (10 liters) of water.

Using a hose to wash the car makes the job easier and more fun. But rinsing with a hose can add up to more than 30 buckets of water. Use buckets of water to wash the car instead. You will use a lot less.

Many children in the developing world walk three to four hours each day to fetch water.

An average adult in the United States uses between 132 and 159 gallons (500 and 600 liters) of water a day. It pours from our faucets. It's clean, safe, and ready to use.

Many people in less-developed countries around the world use only about 24 gallons (90 liters) of water a day. That water might be in a well miles from their home. The water may also be dirty or diseased. About 1.2 billion people in the world today do not have access to clean water.

UNDERSTANDING EARTH'S WATER SUPPLY

Materials needed
- 5-gallon (19-liter) bucket of water
- tablespoon
- dropper
- three clear glasses or jars, labeled A, B, and C

1) Begin with the 5-gallon (19-liter) container of water. That represents all the water on Earth. Measure out 25.5 tablespoons of water into glass A. That is the water frozen in ice caps and glaciers.

2) Measure out 8 tablespoons of water from the bucket and put it into glass B. That represents groundwater.

3) Fill the dropper with water twice and add the water to glass B. That represents the water held in freshwater lakes, ponds, and reservoirs.

4) Measure out a drop of water and add it to glass B. That represents water in rivers and streams.

5) Measure out two drops and add the water to glass B. That represents water in the atmosphere, such as clouds, fog, and rain.

6) Fill the dropper with water twice and add the water to glass C. That represents water held in salt lakes and inland seas.

Look at the bucket and the three glasses. How much of this water is available for humans and animals to use as drinking water?

> **i** Only the water in glass B is available for all living things on Earth to use. If this water is dirty, it must be cleaned up (if possible) before it can be used.

WATER IN DANGER

Chemicals used in factories sometimes escape into rivers. Fertilizers used on farms can wash into freshwater supplies. These pollutants can kill plants and animals. They can ruin precious sources of valuable freshwater.

The more uses we create for water, the more demands we put on the water cycle. Every day, millions of gallons of freshwater are wasted in our homes and in industry. Sometimes sources of freshwater become polluted or dry up due to overuse for irrigation.

Toxic *chemicals in rivers and lakes can kill huge numbers of fish. As big fish eat smaller fish, the toxic chemicals in their bodies become more concentrated and more deadly.*

DESALINATION

Desalination is a process for removing salt from ocean water. It is one way to make freshwater available where it is scarce. Desalination of ocean water is common in places that have limited access to freshwater. One such area is the Middle East, which is mostly desert. Sixty percent of the world's desalination plants are there. As the demand for water increases, this process is growing in other areas of the world. Producing water this way is expensive, however. In places that have plenty of freshwater, it's better to use less water than to look for ways to make it!

WHAT CAN WE DO?

Governments can punish companies that pollute water. Some companies have been forced to pay millions of dollars in fines.

We ALL can save water in our everyday lives. Remember: Only 1 percent of the water on Earth is usable freshwater. If we use Earth's freshwater faster than nature can recycle it, there will not be enough water to go around in the future.

Freshwater is vital to human, animal, and plant life. It is the most valuable resource on Earth, and we must not waste it.

GLOSSARY

accumulation: the process of something building up or collecting. In the water cycle, accumulation is the stage in which water remains for a period of time underground, in the ocean, or in another body of water.

aquifer: a natural underground lake. Water that has seeped into the ground is stored between layers of gravel or permeable rock.

atmosphere: the thick layer of air that surrounds Earth

biome: a large geographical area with similar climate, weather, and plant and animal life. Examples of biomes include rain forests, oceans, and deserts.

condensation: the process in which a gas changes to a liquid

desalination: a process that removes salt from ocean water

drought: an unusually long period without rainfall. Droughts often cause severe water shortages and famine.

elements: substances made up of a single type of atom. Elements can't be broken into simpler components by chemical processes.

erosion: the wearing away of material by water, wind, or glacial ice

evaporation: the process in which a liquid changes to a gas, such as when liquid water turns to water vapor

famine: a severe shortage of food that can lead to starvation and disease

flash flood: a flood that occurs within a few hours of heavy rainfall

freshwater: water that is not salty and that can be used by humans, animals, and plants. The water in ponds, lakes, rivers, and streams is usually freshwater.

glacier: a large body of ice that moves slowly down a slope or valley or spreads out on the surface of the land

global warming: a gradual warming of Earth's atmosphere. Most scientists believe that this is partly caused by humans burning fossil fuels, such as oil and coal.

gravity: the force that pulls objects toward Earth

groundwater: water that has seeped through Earth's surface and is held underground in soil or among rocks

hail: water droplets high in the atmosphere that have frozen. They fall to Earth as small balls of ice.

humidity: a measure of the amount of water vapor in the air

hydroelectric: describes the use of running water to create electricity

iceberg: a large floating mass of ice that has broken away from an glacier

irrigation: the process of bringing water to a place, such as pumping water from a river to irrigate (water) crops

landform: a feature on Earth's surface, such as a mountain

matter: anything that has weight and takes up space. The three states of matter are solid, liquid, and gas.

molecule: a tiny particle that consists of two or more atoms bonded together. It is the smallest part of a substance that has all the characteristics of that substance.

natural resources: the materials, energy sources, and living things found in nature that are useful to people and other living creatures. Water, air, minerals, the Sun's energy, plants, and animals are all natural resources.

organism: All living things are organisms. However, the term is often used to describe very small living creatures, such as bacteria.

permeable: having openings that let liquids or gases pass through

polar ice caps: huge, permanently frozen areas of ice at the North and South poles

pollutant: anything that makes a substance dirty or impure

precipitation: any form of water, such as rain or snow, that falls to Earth's surface

reservoir: a large natural or artificially made lake that is used to store water for supply to homes and businesses

salt water: water, such as ocean water, that contains dissolved salts

sediment: material deposited by water, wind, or glaciers

sleet: a cold, slushy substance halfway between rain and snow. Sleet is caused by snowflakes melting as they fall to Earth because the ground temperature is above freezing.

temperate: having a climate that is mild. It is not too hot or too cold.

toxic: poisonous; harmful to living things

transpiration: the process in which plants give off water vapor through tiny pores in their leaves called stomates

water vapor: a gas that is produced when water evaporates

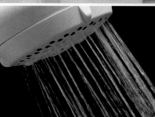